FUN FOODS FOR FUSSY KIDS

English text edited by Jeanette Green

Translated from the French by Kim Allen

English type design by Laura Hammond Hough

Library of Congress Cataloging-in-Publication Data

1 3 5 7 9 10 8 6 4 2

Published by Sterling Publishing Company, Inc.

387 Park Avenue South, New York, N.Y. 10016

© 2001 by Mumu Bienenstock & Mimi Bloch

English translaition © 2002 by Sterling Publishing, Co., Inc.

Originally published by Caramel, Grimbregen, Belgium

under the title *L'Appetit vient en s'amusant*

Distributed in Canada by Sterling Publishing Co., Inc.

Canadian Manda Group. One Atlantic Avenue, Suite 105

Toronto, Ontario, Canada M6K 3E7

Distributed in Great Britain and Europe by Chris Lloyd at

Orca Book Services, Stanley House, Fleets Lane, Poole BH15 3AJ, England

Distributed in Australia by Capricorn Link (Australia) Pty Ltd.

P.O. Box 704 Windsor, NSW 2756 Australia

Printed in China

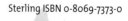

Sterling ISBN 0-8069-7373-0

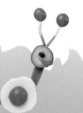

FUN FOODS FOR FUSSY KIDS

Mumu Bienenstock & Mimi Bloch

Sterling Publishing Co., Inc.
New York

CONTENTS

Sweet or Savory: If you use humor and imagination, you'll be able to transform ordinary meals into celebrations, and your child will discover a cornucopia of surprising flavors and taste treats.

With these fun foods, we've devised ways to stimulate kids' appetites and to teach them to eat vegetables, fruits, and much more. Here are some ways: Concoct lovely plates that suggest fun stories they can quickly devour. That way, they'll first eat with their eyes.

You don't have to create difficult or sophisticated recipes. Kids like to eat wholesome and easy-to-munch meals and delicious snacks. We offer ideas to inspire you, but don't worry about substituting one ingredient for another. You know what your kids prefer.

If you don't have time to cook, don't panic. Just use ready-made cakes, cookies, and pizza crusts as a beginning.

Allow kids to participate in food preparation. No matter what their age, there's probably something they could do. Just reserve tasks for yourself that could present danger, such as chopping or cooking. Use your imagination and these fun recipes will soon become favorite meals that you can add to your culinary repertoire.

Bon appétit and have fun…

—Mumu and Mimi

BASIC RECIPES

We've adjusted ingredients in basic recipes for American cooks. Follow the metric measurements if you have a good kitchen scale.

Yellow Vanilla Cake
- 8-inch (20-cm) cake pan, greased
- 1 cup (250 g) butter
- 3/4 cup (200 g) sugar
- 2 1/4 cups (250 g) sifted, self-rising flour
- 4 large eggs
- 1 tablespoon (sachet) vanilla sugar or 1 teaspoon vanilla

Melt the butter in a saucepan over low heat. Pour the melted butter into a bowl with the sugar and vanilla sugar, stirring it in with a wooden spoon. Then add the eggs and the sifted flour and mix well until the batter is creamy and everything is the same consistency. Pour the batter into a greased or buttered cake pan and then bake in a preheated oven for 50 minutes at 325°F (160°C).

For a small, 4-inch (10-cm) cake, use half the recipe, a smaller pan, and reduce baking time. The cake is done when a toothpick placed in the center comes out clean.

Butter Cookies
- 1 cup (125 g) softened butter
- 1/2 cup (120 g) sugar
- 2 eggs
- 1 1/4 cups (150 g) sifted flour
- 1 tablespoon (sachet) vanilla sugar or 1 teaspoon vanilla
- 1 egg yolk for brushing

Mix the softened butter and the sugar in a bowl. Add the eggs, the vanilla sugar (or vanilla), and sifted flour. Blend until the batter is firm and consistent. After allowing it to chill (one hour or more), roll out the dough with a rolling pin, and create shapes with a cookie cutter. Brush the cookies with egg yolk, use a spatula to place them on an ungreased baking sheet, and bake them in a preheated oven for 5–10 minutes at 325°F (160°C).

Crêpes
- 1 cup (250 g) sifted flour
- 3 eggs
- 2 cups (1/2 liter) liquid (half milk, half water)
- pinch of salt
- 2 tablespoons oil
- 1 tablespoon (sachet) vanilla sugar or 1 teaspoon vanilla

Place the flour in a large bowl and pour in the liquid, stirring as you pour in order to avoid lumps. When this mixture is blended well, add the beaten eggs, and then add the oil, salt, and sugar. Mix thoroughly and allow the batter to sit in the refrigerator at least one hour before using. Pour the batter onto a medium-hot grill. Turn over the crêpe after one side creates tiny bubbles.

Lemon Icing
- 1 3/4 cup (200 g) sifted confectioner's sugar
- 1 egg white
- a few drops of lemon

Mix the three ingredients well with a wooden spoon until you get a creamy, consistent batter. For colored icing, add one or two drops of food coloring and blend well. Use a spatula to uniformly spread the icing. If the topping is still transparent when you spread it on your cakes, allow it to harden 15 minutes, and then spread on a second layer.

Chocolate Glaze

Melt 8 ounces (200 g) of chocolate over low heat (in a double boiler, if you have one) with a small amount of water. Mix well to obtain a smooth and creamy glaze or topping.

DECORATING TIPS

How to Work with Marzipan

Rolled Icing or Marzipan Sheets

Mix natural-colored marzipan with a few drops of food coloring and work it in until you have a dough that's all the same color.

Place the marzipan between two sheets of plastic wrap and roll it out a few times with a rolling pin to create a smooth sheet. The more you roll, the more the dough thins out and becomes larger.

Coloring

Tint the marzipan with a few drops of food coloring. The subtlety of the color depends on the number of drops. Often less is best, but your child might like knock-out color.

The more color you add, the darker the marzipan will become (for pale pink: use only one to two drops of red).

To lighten it, add more natural-colored marzipan. To create new colors, mix two pieces of different colors (a piece of yellow mixed with a piece of red makes orange marzipan).

Striped Sheet

To create horizontal bands, prepare sausage-shaped rolls of marzipan. Using your hands, place them between two sheets of plastic wrap, and roll out a few times with a rolling pin to obtain long bands.

To join them in a striped sheet, cut the edges and combine them again (always between plastic wrap), then roll them out one more time with a rolling pin.

Figurines

To create fun figurines, work the marzipan as you would Play-Dough. Sculpt easy, simple forms and have fun putting them together, letting your imagination run free.

Tools

To create lovely decorations, use little, practical tools, like toothpicks, knives, molds, glasses, cookie cutters, scissors, rolling pin, and spatulas. But use your hands and work your fingers for the final touches. As you get the hang of it yourself, you may want to invite kids to try.

We've graded these recipes from the very easy to the toughest.

 Very Easy to Make   Easy to Make    You'll need to concentrate a little.

 This lets you know how long each dish takes.

MY SWEET

AT THE MARKET

- Ready-to-use tart shell
- Apricot compote or jam
- Peaches
- Strawberries
- Raspberries
- Lime
- Blueberries
- Pink grapefruit

30 min.

IN YOUR KITCHEN

1

Wash the fruit well. With a sharp knife, cut the citrus fruits (lime and grapefruit) into slices. For the lion's mane, make several slices of lime and arrange them in a circle. Place the round slice of pink grapefruit on top of the lime slices. In the center of the grapefruit, put half a peach for the lion's nose and mouth.

2

To make the lion's face, use blueberries for eyes, a raspberry for the nose, a strawberry cut in two for ears, thin slices of orange zest for whiskers, and a small slice of strawberry for the mouth.

3

For the lion's paws, cut a half peach in two and use a small bit of orange peel for the tail. For the lion's body, fill the tart shell with apricot compote. Arrange all parts to form a pretty lion.

LION

OLD-FASHIONED

AT THE MARKET

- Long sandwich roll or sandwich bread
- Cheese
- Carrot purée
- Cherry tomatoes
- 1 carrot
- 1 cucumber
- Dill or chives
- 1 snow pea
- Ear of baby corn

30 min.

IN YOUR KITCHEN

1

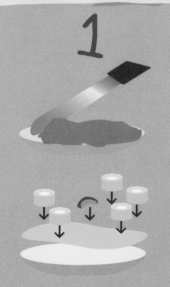

Wash the raw vegetables. Quickly blanch the baby corn and the snow pea.

Cut the sandwich roll or bread lengthwise. Garnish one with carrot puree and the other with a slice of cheese. Then add slices of baby corn and pieces of tomato.

2

Lay out the two bread pieces to form the engine's body and main smokestack. The bread cut in half makes the base of the smokestack and the other the locomotive's body. Cover the connection with a snow pea.

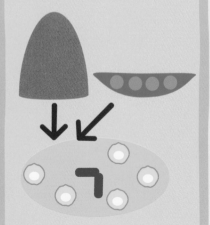

3

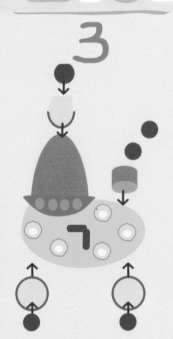

Finish the main smokestack and lay out the small rear smokestack with slices of carrot, tomato halves, a piece of cucumber, and use a bunch of dill for smoke. Make the wheels and other details with the cucumber, tomato, or corn.

LOCOMOTIVE SANDWICH

FRUIT-COMPOTE

AT THE MARKET

- Large sweet bread slices
- Red fruit compote or jam
- Apricot compote or jam
- Golden grapes
- Strawberries
- Red apple
- Green apple
- Lime
- Blueberries

40 min.

IN YOUR KITCHEN

1

Cut the slices of bread into simple shapes: a rectangle for the trailer's body and a trapezoid for the roof. Assemble them. Generously spread the bread slices with jam.

2

Wash the fruit. Cut the strawberries in two and lay them out carefully to create the tiles of the trailer's roof.

3

For the wheels, stack slices of lemon, apples, and strawberries on top of each other. For the rest, add a touch of imagination...

TRAILER

LUNCH-MUNCH

At the Market

- Small pita, focaccia, or flat sourdough bread round

- Small round roll

- Ham

- Red and green lettuce leaves

- Cucumber

- Orange or red pepper

- 2 olives

- Radish

30 min.

In Your Kitchen

1

Cut the bread in half horizontally. Wash the vegetables. Garnish the sandwich, buttering it first (or use mayonnaise or mustard), with a layer of green lettuce, topped with a layer of ham, and scatter pieces of red lettuce leaves for garnish.

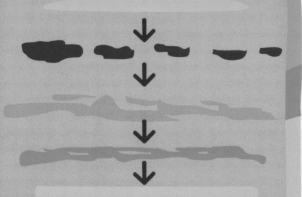

2

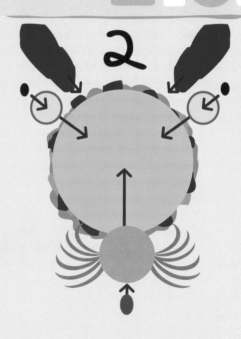

Put the second half of bread on top to make a sandwich. Add crunchy details to shape the bunny: a small roll for the muzzle, two cucumber slices and olives for eyes, pepper strips for whiskers, a radish slice for the mouth, several leaves of red lettuce for the long ears. Use your imagination to make the bunny appetizing and attractive!

BUNNY

CUTE AS A BUG...

At the Market

- Cookie dough (see page 6)

- Yellow icing (see page 6)

- Natural-colored marzipan

- Blue marzipan (see page 7)

- Licorice laces

- Black candies

45 min.

In Your Kitchen

1

Roll out the cookie dough with a rolling pin and place it in a greased cake pan to form a nice round shape.

Bake the cookie in a preheated oven at 350°F (180°C) for 5 to 10 minutes.

Generously top the cooled cookie with yellow icing and wait until it is fully dry before decorating it. Then cover the shape with the long broad strips of blue marzipan.

2

For the head, roll out a small piece of natural-colored marzipan, formed into a half-circle, and decorate it with licorice laces to create the antennae and the mouth. For the eyes, put small balls of marzipan on each side of the head, gently flatten them, and top them with two candies. For the feet (real insects have six legs and spiders have eight), a few more licorice laces will work very well.

WELL, INSECT

SOMETHING

- Crêpe batter (see page 6)
- White cheese (goat cheese, cream cheese, feta, ricotta, Edam)
- Salmon
- Carrots
- Olives
- Cucumber
- Radishes
- Lime
- Chives
- Cherry tomatoes

60 min.

IN YOUR KITCHEN

1

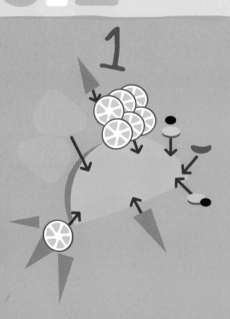

Prepare the crêpes in a frying pan, fill them with white cheese, and fold them in half. Use thin slices of salmon and lime to delicately cover most of the top of the first crêpe. Add slices of radishes and olives for eyes and a zest of tomato for the mouth. Use triangular slices of carrot for the tail and fins.

2

Decorate the second crêpe with slices of radish and cucumber. Add an olive on a slice of radish for the eye, a cherry tomato for the nose, and chives for fins. Form a tail with cucumber slices cut in half.

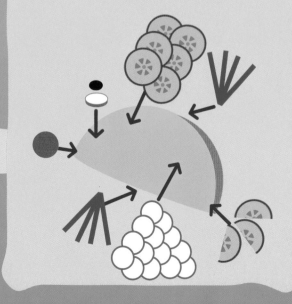

FISHY CRÊPES

HOW, NOW, BROWN

- Large cake (8-inch or 20-cm; see page 6)
- Small cake (4-inch or 10-cm, see page 6; or buy one)
- Coconut
- Grated chocolate or chocolate sprinkles
- Honey
- Chocolate pastilles
- Chocolate ice-cream cones
- Green licorice laces
- Pink marzipan (see page 7), rolled out
- Round pink candies

60 min.

In Your Kitchen

1

Cut the small round cake into two and place the two halves on each side of the large round cake, making big, beautiful cow ears.

2

Generously cover all cakes with honey. Sprinkle coconut on one ear and half the cow's face and granulated chocolate on the other ear and half face.

3

Using the template from page 45, make her cute muzzle out of rolled marzipan. Finish the cow's face with chocolate pastilles for eyes, small ice-cream cones for horns, and round pink candies for nostrils. Don't forget the green licorice laces to make the grass in its hungry mouth.

& WHITE COW

SAUSAGE

- Ready-to-use savory tartlets
- Round toasts
- Small sausages
- Mustard
- Ketchup
- Carrot
- Raisins

20 min.

In Your Kitchen

1

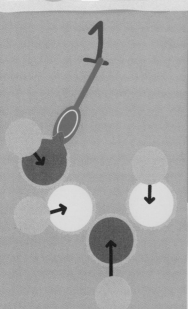

Fill the tartlets with mustard and ketchup and place a small round toast in the middle of each. Place these one after the other in alternating colors to create a cute body.

2

For the face, use two raisins for eyes, a half sausage for the nose, a thin slice of carrot for the mouth, and sausages for the antennae.

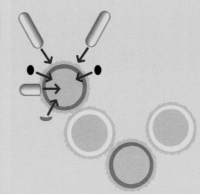

3

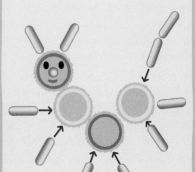

Add several feet and a tail made out of lots of sausages. Don't be afraid to be inventive! The more comical it is, the more your little gourmet will ask for this little creature again...

CATERPILLAR

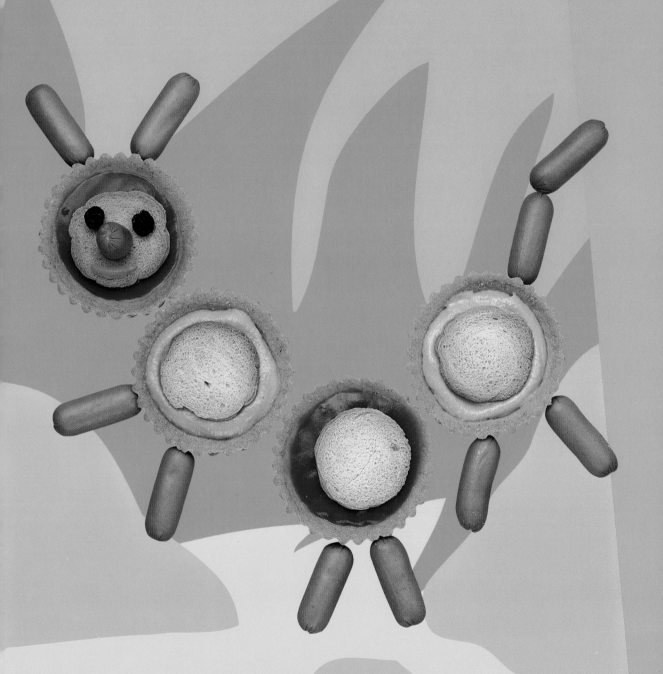

PUPPET-SHOW

60 min.

AT THE MARKET

- Orange-filled sandwich cookies
- Chocolate sticks
- Marzipan in blue, orange, red, yellow, brown, white (see page 7)
- Assortment of candy

IN YOUR KITCHEN

1

Cover the cookies with marzipan, each a different color.

2

Inspired by the models on page 25, with your hands, sculpt simple shapes: circles for heads, different sizes of rectangles for cars, triangles for bow ties, hats or cockscombs, a cone and circle for ice cream.

3

Decorate the figures with miniature candies and add little details for personality and to make them recognizable. Push a small chocolate stick into each cookie and play puppet show before gobbling them up.

CANDY

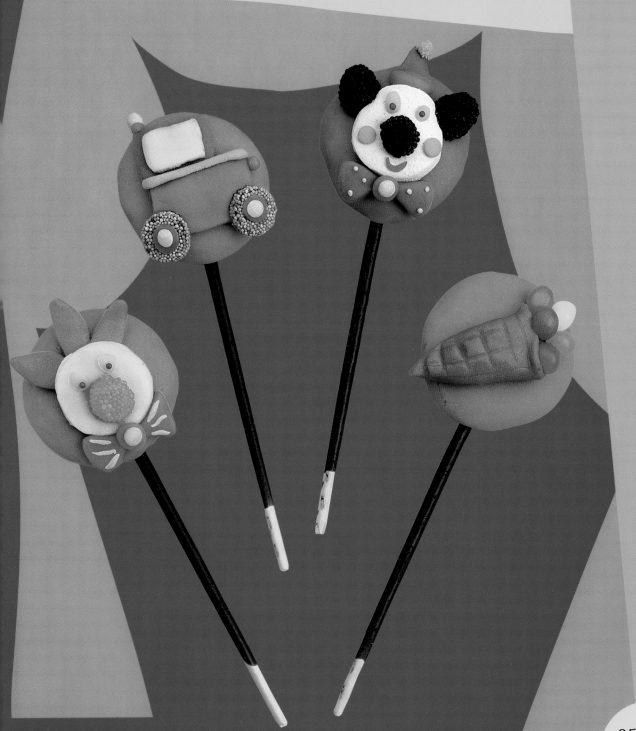

TROPICAL

At the Market

- Ready-to-use pizza crust
- Tomato puree
- Mozzarella cheese slices
- Tomatoes
- Olives
- Zucchini
- Orange peppers
- Chives

40 min.

In Your Kitchen

1

Wash all the vegetables. Preheat the oven for 10 minutes at 400°F (200°C).

Spread the tomato paste as uniformly as possible on the pizza crust for the face.

2

Use pieces of mozzarella and olives for eyes, tomatoes cut in half for cheeks, a cute little tomato for the nose, a thin slice of pepper for the mouth, and thin slices of zucchini for hair.

3

Bake for about five minutes at 350°F (180°C). Finish off decorating with a slice of mozzarella and thin slices of pepper for the tropical hat and silly ears.

Invent other objects: an alarm clock, a ball, sun... Your kids will enjoy these little culinary surprises and eat them in a wink.

PIZZA HEAD

SHEEP PICKING

- Cake (see page 6)
- Chocolate glaze (see page 6)
- Marzipan in green, red, pink, and brown (see page 7)
- Honey
- Coconut
- Green licorice laces
- Grated chocolate or chocolate sprinkles
- Small green candies

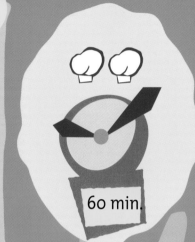

60 min.

IN YOUR KITCHEN

1

Ice the cake with chocolate glaze and add chocolate sprinkles. For the sheep, model pink marzipan: ovals for the head, ears, and body; sausage shapes for legs. (See template on page 44.) Flatten them slightly. Use little balls and candies for eyes and nose. Sprinkle coconut over honey on the body.

2

For the apple tree, put the marzipan between two sheets of plastic wrap and flatten it out with a rolling pin to create a good sheet. Cut out the tree shape, using the template on page 44.

3

Model red balls for apples. Insert a chocolate sprinkle or piece of grated chocolate for the stem. Flatten tiny balls of green marzipan for leaves and carve them with a knife. Make the ladder with green licorice laces. Assemble everything, and lightly sprinkle the orchard ground with miniature candies.

APPLES

AMERICAN

- Carrot purée
- Carrots
- Snow peas
- Ear of baby corn
- Cherry tomato
- Cucumber
- Round toasts
- Black olives
- Small plate

20 min.

IN YOUR KITCHEN

1

Wash the vegetables well. Quickly blanch the snow peas and carrots in water or in the microwave. Uniformly spread the carrot purée in the small plate; then cut the vegetables in two or into slices.

2

For the face, use bits of cucumber for eyebrows; toasts topped with cucumber rounds and tomato halves and olives for eyes, a baby corn cut in two for the nose, and slices of cucumber for the mouth.

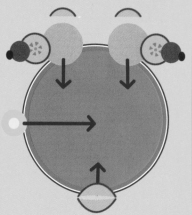

3

For the feather headdress, use thin slices of carrots and snow peas.

For the necklace, arrange cucumber rounds and snow peas. You've transformed a boring carrot purée into a character ready for adventures!

SWEET DREAMS,

AT THE MARKET

- Cake (see page 6)

- Natural-colored marzipan

- Blue, pink, yellow, red, and orange marzipan (see page 7)

- Small candies

60 min.

IN YOUR KITCHEN

1

Place the blue marzipan between two sheets of plastic wrap and roll it out with a rolling pin to create a nice sheet. Use the rolled marzipan to cover the cake. Prepare the yellow marzipan in the same way, and cut it into a half-moon and put it over the blue marzipan to create the folded blanket edge.

2

For marzipan rabbits, sculpt with your fingers simple shapes: a trapezoid for the torso, a ball for the head, two flat oval or round sheets for ears, small balls and mini-sausage shapes for hands, sausage shapes for arms, a small ball for the nose, and more. Assemble everything.

3

Add the small, sweet details and then attach the rabbits to the cake. Don't forget the feet (flat ovals) and hat (a cone on a flat circle).

BUNNY BABY

TEDDY BEAR

- Round sandwich bread
- Carrot purée
- Zucchini
- Chives
- Cucumber
- 2 raisins
- Tomato
- Ear of baby corn

20 min.

IN YOUR KITCHEN

1

Wash the vegetables. Take two slices of bread and cover them with carrot purée. Quickly blanch the zucchini and baby corn in water or in the microwave.

2

Use raisins for eyes, a bit of cucumber for the nose, a thin slice of tomato for the mouth, round slices of zucchini cut in two for the feet and ears, and a bow tie made of chives and a slice of baby corn.

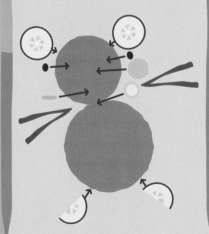

3

In the blink of an eye, our little teddy bear becomes lovable. If you would rather make a little pig, substitute carrot purée with a light pink roe or cleaned and cooked baby shrimp...

34

VEGGIE SANDWICH

TRAIN

At the Market

- Marzipan in pink, red, yellow, blue, green, orange (see page 7)
- Miniature candies
- Cute candies

60 min.

In Your Kitchen

1

To create this cute little train that can scale a mountain, prepare two blocks out of marzipan and a smaller piece of marzipan shaped in a half-moon for the conductor's cabin. Surround the bottom of the engine (the car where the conductor sits) and the car behind him with marzipan wheels. Assemble the two train cars.

2

For the pig (engineer or conductor), use your hands to sculpt the torso (a trapezoid), the head (a very round ball), the nose (a very small, slightly flattened ball), the ears (two flat circles), and the arms (two sausage shapes). Assemble everything to form a sweet engineer! Add candy details to make the eyes, mouth, bow tie, and more...

3

For the frog (passenger), make a trapezoid for the body, a large ball for the head (make an opening for the mouth and place inside it a small red ball for the tongue), two balls at the top of the head for froggy eyes, decorated with disks, and two long sausage shapes for arms.

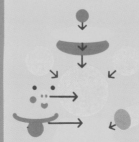

RIDE

VEGGIE

AT THE MARKET

- Cucumber
- Carrots
- Radishes
- Ears of baby corn
- Chunks of Gruyere cheese
- Chives
- Mint leaves
- Toothpicks

60 min.

IN YOUR KITCHEN

1

Wash the vegetables well and blanch the carrots and the ears of baby corn.

For the airplane, make a rectangular cut in a piece of cucumber and scoop it out with a spoon. Using toothpicks to hold them in place, add airplane wings (carrots cut lengthwise) and the propeller (ears of baby corn). Construct the control-panel dials with rounds of carrot and baby corn.

2

For the pilot and passenger, prepare chunks of cheese for the body, radishes cut in two for arms, a radish for the head, chives or mint leaves for hair, and round slices of carrot placed on top of each other for hats.

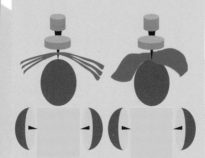

3

Have fun assembling all ingredients and putting the passengers in the plane. Don't forget to remove the toothpicks before eating the decorations.

AIRPLANE

FRUIT

AT THE MARKET

- Lime
- Pear
- Banana
- Black grapes
- Star fruit
- Kiwi
- Raspberry
- Blueberries
- Toothpicks
- Wooden skewers

45 min.

IN YOUR KITCHEN

1

Wash the fruit. With a sharp knife, carefully peel the kiwi and banana and cut them into rounds.

2

For the clown's legs, thread slices of star fruit, kiwi, banana, and grapes on the wooden skewers and stick them into the body (the standing pear). Make the arms the same way: three grapes and a slice of banana will do nicely.

3

Fasten the head (a lime) with a toothpick and prepare thin slices of star fruit to make ears for this silly clown. Finish the face with blueberries for eyes and a raspberry for the nose. Add a bit of imagination to make this character cute.

CLOWN

AT THE MARKET

- Marzipan in pink, red, white, yellow, blue, green, orange, brown (see page 7)

- Miniature candies

- Marzipan strips in many colors (see page 7)

60 min.

IN YOUR KITCHEN

1

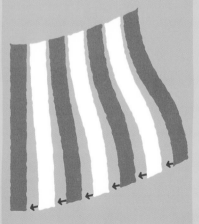

Combine strips of marzipan in various colors to make a striped beach towel.

2

Create the beach girl using mostly your fingers. Model a round ball for the head, sausage shapes for limbs, a large flat trapezoid for the beach dress, very thin sausage shapes for hair, and add sausage shapes for the hat and at the dress hem.

3

To assemble the bathing beauty, place her dress on the beach towel and curve it up to affix the head and arms and to slip the slightly bent legs underneath. Add all little details (like polka dots or a hat). Let the model inspire you to create something new of your own.

VACATION

SWEET

Templates for Marzipan & Other Shapes

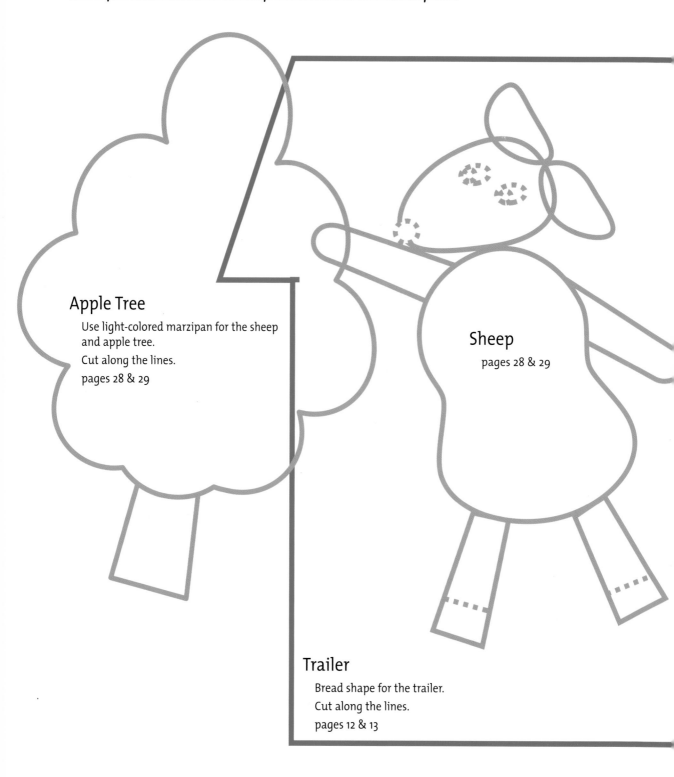

Apple Tree

Use light-colored marzipan for the sheep and apple tree.

Cut along the lines.

pages 28 & 29

Sheep

pages 28 & 29

Trailer

Bread shape for the trailer.

Cut along the lines.

pages 12 & 13

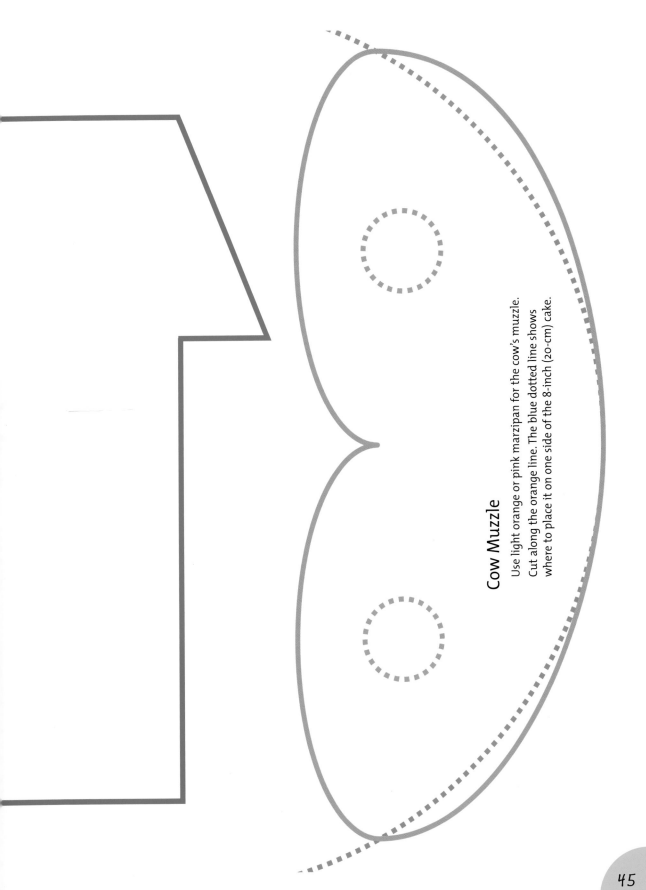

Cow Muzzle

Use light orange or pink marzipan for the cow's muzzle. Cut along the orange line. The blue dotted line shows where to place it on one side of the 8-inch (20-cm) cake.

Notes

INDEX